GORILLA Journal

By
Carolyn Franklin

BOOK HOUSE

RWANDA PAYS DES MILLE COLLINES

Africa

Bwindi Impenetrable National Park

Sarambwe ●

Buhoma ●

Ruhija ●

UGANDA

Gorillas. Rwanda.

1 3 5 7 9 8 6 4 2

A CIP catalogue record for this book is available from the British Library.

HB ISBN-13: 978-1-906370-57-2
PB ISBN-13: 978-1-906370-59-6

Printed and bound in China.
Printed on paper from sustainable sources.

Visit our website at **www.salariya.com**
for **free** electronic versions of:
You Wouldn't Want to be an Egyptian Mummy!
You Wouldn't Want to be a Roman Gladiator!
Avoid Joining Shackleton's Polar Expedition!
Avoid Sailing on a 19th-Century Whaling Ship!

PUBLISHED BY BOOK HOUSE 25 MARLBOROUGH PLACE, BRIGHTON

Consultant: John Cooper

Photo credits:
Anna Chippendale,
Dreamstime, Fotolia, iStockphoto,
Jonathan Salariya

Published in Great Britain in 2009
by
Book House, an imprint of
The Salariya Book Company Ltd,
25 Marlborough Place, Brighton,
BNI IUB
www.salariya.com
www.book-house.co.uk

PAPER FROM
SUSTAINABLE
FORESTS

Contents

What to take

I started planning this trip to Rwanda just over a year ago, when I first heard about the amazing gorillas that live there in the mountains. Since then I have found out all about these gorillas and their environment. Very few mountain gorillas still survive in the wild, and I want to see if I can do anything to help them.

My flight will take me to Rwanda in East Africa. The gorillas live in north-west Rwanda near the border with the Democratic Republic of the Congo.

CHECKLIST

- Passport and visa
- Flight tickets
- Medication
- Maps and directions
- Local money
- Notebook
- Phrasebook

Rwanda

Africa

Kikagatu

Uganda

Rutshuru   Kabale

Kisoro

Democratic
Republic of
the Congo

Ruhengeri   Gabiro
Byumba

Kivuruga

Goma

Rwanda

Gisenyi   **Kigali**   Rwamagana

Lake
Kivu

Kibuye   Gitarama

Gako   Kibungo

Ngara

Gikongoro

Cyangugu   Kigerne   Butare   **Burundi**   **Tanzania**

4

Rwanda

Discover a new Africa

WHAT TO PACK

Waterproof rucksack

Hat and sunglasses

Waterproof walking boots

Long trousers x 4

Long-sleeved shirts x 4

Socks and underwear x 12

Fleece   * Sunscreen
     * Insect repellent

Water bottle

Camera, memory cards & charger

Binoculars

Sketch pad, pencils, watercolours
brushes and eraser

Preparation: I need to be fit because the altitude makes you tired (less oxygen in the air)! See doctor for injections/tablets required.
* (Note: mountain gorillas live too high up for most malaria-carrying mosquitoes or so I've been told!)

I've arrived!

Wednesday 6th May

I have hardly slept for excitement since we arrived. Up at 5 A.M! A quick breakfast and then we set off. After a very bumpy, muddy ride in a jeep we arrive at the lower slopes of Mount Bisoke where the Amahoro group of gorillas live.

The volcanoes are where the gorillas live.

There are five extinct volcanoes in the Virunga conservation area. Mount Bisoke is one of them.

6 A.M. - all aboard the jeep!

Route to the reserve

We've been told that we might see some forest elephants, buffaloes, giant forest hogs, bushpigs, bushbucks, black-fronted duikers, spotted hyenas, and my particular favourite - golden monkeys - all on our way to the reserve. I'll keep my camera and binoculars ready at all times!

Democratic Republic of the Congo

Virunga Volcanoes

Uganda

Gahina
3,474 m

Mahabura
4,127 m

Bisoke
3,711 m

Karasimbi
4,507 m

Volcanoes National Park

Ruhengeri

＊ Our camp!

0   5 km

View of the Parc National des Volcans

(Volcanoes National Park)

Farhani's name means 'happy' in the Kinyarwandan language.

8 A.M: Meet Farhani

Farhani will be our guide. He briefs us about how we should behave and what we can expect to see on our trek.
＊Note: See 'Guidelines for meeting the gorillas' on page 9.

View of the
forest where the
gorillas live

Thursday 7th May

Mountain trekking

We've been trekking for just over an hour now,
and I feel short of breath because there is less
oxygen in the air at this altitude. I keep slipping
and sliding on the muddy slopes, and I nearly fell
into a bank of stinging nettles. I've been stung by
ants and, despite my long trousers, I've been
badly scratched by thorns! Suddenly Farhani
stops and points. Gorilla poo! Almost at once
we see movement in the trees up ahead and hear
loud, grunting calls.

Guidelines for meeting the gorillas

* Don't visit the gorillas if you have a cold, flu or any contagious illness that could spread to them.
* Don't go closer than 7 metres.
* Spend no longer than an hour with them.
* Maximum of 8 people per group.
* Do not spit in the park.
* If you need to cough, cover your mouth and turn away.
* While near the gorillas, keep your voice low, and move slowly.
* If a gorilla charges or makes warning sounds at you, don't be alarmed. Stand still, look away from the gorilla and wait for your guide's instructions.

Hard work - but lots of fun!

10.30 A.M: Spot gorilla dung

Poo!

This grasshopper jumped onto my sketch pad!

9

Nose prints of the Murisanga group

JANJA	𐰧	female
LESSENJINA	𐰧	female
MAAISHO	𐰧	baby
KAMPANGA	⋎	female
GANEANGI	⋁	baby
SHINDA	⋰	male
KAMBA	⋎	male

I've quickly sketched in the shapes of some of the gorillas' 'nose prints'. Farhani told me they were all different and could be used to identify each individual.

This family group is made up of nine animals. There are four females, three babies and two males.

Thursday 7th May
First sighting

I'll never forget my first sighting of a gorilla. We sensed a strong, powerful animal smell, and then we heard the sound of something large moving through the trees. Suddenly only 8 metres away stood a magnificent young male – a blackback gorilla.

He was one of the Amahoro gorillas. Farhani told us that he was eating giant celery. He seemed quite content to have us nearby while he ate. We watched in fascination.

(Amahoro means 'peace' in the local Kinyarwanda language.)

A gorilla's average day consists of foraging for food in the early morning, followed by a late morning rest. Then it forages for more food in the afternoon. At night the gorillas take a well-deserved rest.

10.46 A.M. Gorilla eating!

Originally the group was larger, but fighting between rival silverback gorillas split it into two new, smaller families.

NOTE: Farhani told us not to point. Apparently gorillas don't like it!

Close encounter

Friday 8th May, 3.15 P.M.

There's more movement in the trees, and another gorilla arrives in the clearing. It's an older male - a large silverback. The young male retreats. The silverback looks agitated by us. He beats his chest and charges towards us. We back up nervously into some nettles and Farhani calms the big silverback by making grunting noises until he backs off.

Large silverback!

Mountain gorillas are some of the largest living primates. Standing upright, the average silverback is 1.73 metres tall, has an arm span of 2.29 metres and weighs an astonishing 204–227 kilograms! Male gorillas usually weigh twice as much as females.

HANDS AND FEET

Hand

Foot

Ideal for hanging on!

Gorillas walk on all fours, using their feet and the knuckles of their hands to support their weight. But in a chest-beating charge, a male gorilla may run on two legs for up to 6 metres. Ours did! (The hair stands up on the back of my neck as I write this.)

Gorillas' hands are similar to ours: they have five fingers, including their thumb. Each foot has five toes, including a big toe. Gorillas can grasp things with their hands or their feet.

The forest

The rainforest where the gorillas live is full of many different types of plants and trees. Temperatures and rainfall change as you go higher, so vegetation growing at the base of the mountain is different from that found at the top.

I was wondering how gorillas drink. Farhani explained that they get most of the water they need from their food and from dew on the leaves. However, when a gorilla is thirsty it soaks the fur on the back of its hand and sucks the water from it.

Bamboo thicket

playing in the trees!

Saturday 9th May

We saw some young gorillas playing up in the trees. Adult gorillas rarely climb trees, although females will do so in search of fruit. Farhani says that silverbacks occasionally forage in trees, but only if the branches are strong enough to take their weight!

A massive forest millipede - about 10 centimetres long. It's not squidgy - it's hard!

Our camp

Farhani suggests we come back again tomorrow. It's mid-afternoon by the time we get back to camp and I'm exhausted but thrilled! I can't forget the gorillas' eyes - they are brownish-black, with such a look of gentle intelligence. Seeing a gorilla in the wild is an utterly amazing experience. Its enormous size and power suprised me; its black fur is so thick, and its huge hands are so like a human's!

There are so many fascinating insects in the forest. I almost missed this stick insect as it was so cleverly camouflaged on a nearby branch.

Stick insect

15

Gorillas grooming

Sunday 10th May

It's mid-morning now, and we are back with the gorillas again. A large blackback, moving through the forest, leads us to the rest of the group, which is busy feeding. The silverback is lying on his stomach, grooming a youngster. A baby gorilla is perched on his back, watching; it's an incredibly peaceful and moving scene.

Grooming is important to the gorillas. Not only does it help to keep their fur clean and free of insects and parasites, but it also reinforces social bonds.

Silverback grooming youngster

The silverback is using his fingers and teeth to comb through the young gorilla's fur. The youngster seems so relaxed that he is almost in a trance!

Gorillas spend much of their time eating: mostly a variety of plants along with a few insects, and occasionally worms. Adult males can eat up to 34 kilograms of vegetation a day, while a female can eat as much as 18 kilograms.

Thistle leaf

Gorillas feeding

About 20 minutes later, Farhani quietly tells us all to stay very still, and we watch as the entire Amahoro group disappears. It is almost impossible to see them now, as they have climbed high up to feed inside the branches of a vine-covered tree. Farhani says that no tree can last long with nine gorillas in it!

Chomping wild celery

Family groups

Monday 11th May

It's so funny watching the young gorillas play. They seem to be tickling each other and rolling about. One mother gently kisses her baby before she picks it up and moves off into the jungle.

Blackback

I asked Farhani how old the blackback was. He told me that male gorillas between the ages of six and ten are called blackbacks. They keep their black hair colour all over at this stage.

Each group is led by a
dominant silverback who can
weigh up to 227 kilograms.
He is always in charge,
deciding when his family
should wake, rest, eat or sleep.

We hear the gorillas calling to
each other. Hidden by thick
vegetation, they communicate by
sound. The silverback has
about 16 different calls. Some
calls warn of danger; another
may indicate a stranger's presence,
or that there is food nearby.

Silverback

19

Mothers and babies

10 minutes later...

To my astonishment a female walks right in front of us, carrying her baby. The baby is so tiny, it must be newly born. I hold my breath as she passes, standing perfectly still so that I won't disturb her. I take this wondeful photograph of them. The mother is incredibly tender and trusting. Further away, two young gorillas are swinging on vines.

Very inquisitive — he keeps peeping out from behind the leave

Newborn gorillas are small, covered with black hair, and weigh about 2.3 kilograms. They need constant care. Farhani tells us that by the time they are two years old they can reach and chew on vines and branches. They develop about twice as fast as human babies.

A gorilla mother first carries her baby by holding it carefully to her chest. Once the baby can crawl, it will be allowed to explore a bit. The mother will then carry it on her back. Baby gorillas develop quickly from this point on, and will soon seek out playmates. Although weaned at about two years of age, a young gorilla will sleep in its mother's nest for a further year.

Sitting among the vines...

Gorillas are only active for part of the day, building nests in different locations each evening. I took this photograph of the gorillas relaxing in the last of the afternoon's sunshine.

Gorillas' nests
Tuesday 12th May

It is late afternoon and Farhani says that we might see a gorilla building its nest, if we're lucky. We watch the gorillas from a distance as they move about in the forest, eating leaves. Then a young gorilla heads towards us, collecting small branches from nearby bushes. I can't believe it – we are actually about to see a gorilla constructing its nest!

Family group of ground-nesting gorillas

Nests are mainly made from branches, and can be on the ground or in the trees. Smaller, lighter gorillas usually nest in the trees and heavier gorillas nest on the ground - which is lucky, as it meant I could sketch this family.

After about 3 years, young gorillas move out of their mother's nest and build their own. Gorilla groups spend about 40 per cent of their time resting, 30 per cent eating, and the remaining 30 per cent on the move.

This gorilla is unsure of us and seems to be watching to see whether we're friendly or not.

Gorilla behaviour

Farhani explained that gorilla behaviour is as varied as our own. They can be just as curious, bored or annoyed as we can. They show pleasure, excitement, fear and anxiety, too. They can be hostile, of course, but they seem thoughtful and affectionate within the family group.

Gorillas communicate with each other in different ways. For example: noises that sound like stomach rumbles can be a sign of contentment; a series of grunts is a sign of disapproval; roaring is a sign of aggression; and they will scream when threatened.

Rival silverbacks hoot at each other. They beat their chests, thrash nearby trees and often strut about. If a gorilla is afraid, a powerful odour comes from its glands.

Hooting!

Chest beating!

Tuesday 12th May (continued)

On our way back to camp we pass some buffaloes grazing by the roadside. I was suprised to learn that buffaloes are quite capable of defending themselves against a lion, and can even kill it.

Oxpecker

I keep noticing little birds perched on the buffaloes' backs. They are called oxpeckers. They eat the ticks and blood-sucking flies that live off the buffalo's blood - so they are quite welcome guests!

Gorilla habitat
Wednesday 13th May

The gorillas have moved on and it takes Farhani longer to find them today. They are further up the mountain in a bamboo forest, searching for fresh shoots.

Gorillas will normally travel up to 1 kilometre a day, which means (if we are lucky) we should be able to follow them.

Senecio tree *

Gorillas' nest *

Bamboo forest *

First sighting *

Our camp *

Baby gorillas in bamboo forest

Farhani told us that gorilla groups roam within an area which is called their 'home range'. If food sources are spread far apart, then the home range will be quite big. However, if there is plenty of food they won't roam so far. Nevertheless, gorillas can and will cover great distances to get to their favourite plants.

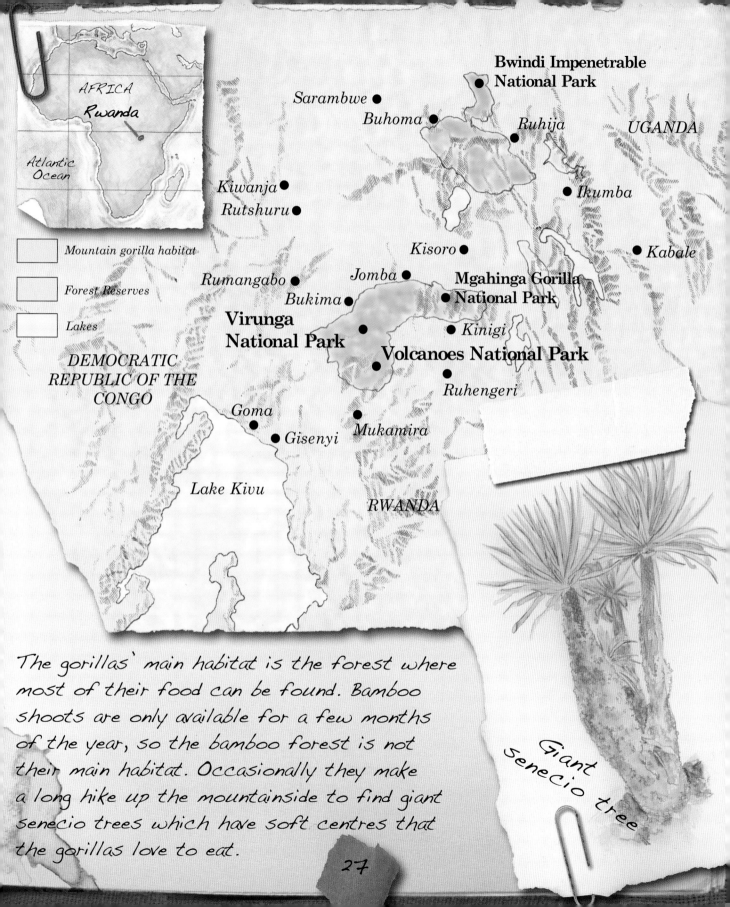

AFRICA
Rwanda

Atlantic Ocean

Bwindi Impenetrable National Park

Sarambwe ●

Buhoma ●

Ruhija ●

UGANDA

Kiwanja ●

Rutshuru ●

Ikumba ●

Kabale ●

Kisoro ●

Mountain gorilla habitat

Forest Reserves

Lakes

Rumangabo ●

Jomba ●

Mgahinga Gorilla National Park

Bukima ●

Virunga National Park

Kinigi ●

Volcanoes National Park

DEMOCRATIC REPUBLIC OF THE CONGO

Ruhengeri ●

Goma ●

Gisenyi ●

Mukamira ●

Lake Kivu

RWANDA

The gorillas' main habitat is the forest where most of their food can be found. Bamboo shoots are only available for a few months of the year, so the bamboo forest is not their main habitat. Occasionally they make a long hike up the mountainside to find giant senecio trees which have soft centres that the gorillas love to eat.

Giant senecio tree

27

Deforestation means that gorillas lose both their home and their source of food.

I must remember when I return home to look up the website of the International Gorilla Conservation Programme at www.igcp.org

Cutting down the trees!

Gorillas in danger

Having seen these beautiful, intelligent and sensitive animals for myself, I cannot bear to think that they are endangered and may not survive. Farhani explained that the mountain gorillas' main threat comes from deforestation. Land is either cleared for agricultural use, or the trees are cut down for firewood.

Disease is another threat. Gorillas are closely related to humans, which makes them vulnerable to many of the same diseases. Unfortunately they don't have our immune system. Any human contact is potentially harmful, even life-threatening.

28

Poaching, too, is a threat to the survival of mountain gorillas. Snares are set to catch other animals like antelope, but sometimes the snares kill or injure gorillas instead. Baby gorillas get caught in them, too.

Other threats come from dealers who commission hunters to capture baby gorillas to sell on to private zoos. War and political unrest in the area also affect these peaceful animals.

Orphaned gorilla being bottle-fed

WAR threatens mountain gorillas

Fighting between Rwanda's ethnic Hutu-led government and Tutsi rebels began claiming gorilla lives in the early 1990s. At least 18 died as Hutu militiamen, charged in the country's 1994 genocide, fled to the Congo and began mounting attacks ack across the border. This conflict, d the related war in Congo, drove any of the gorillas' human ghbours into the National Park to e or look for food. Soon gorillas an dying of human diseases like sles and flu, and at least one rback male was killed and eaten ngry rebels.

After the war, many

landmines in the National Park pose a serious threat to the orillas. The Internationa onservation qui

Four mountain gorillas shot dead in Congo park

A family of four rare mountain gorillas, including a pregnant female, have been shot dead in the Virunga National Park in eastern Democratic Republic f Congo, the World Wide Fund For Nature (WWF) said Thursday.

What can we do?

The good news is that the number of gorillas is growing. Family groups are monitored and great care is taken to stop poachers from reaching them. The parks are regularly patrolled to ensure the gorillas' safety. More people are becoming aware of the need to conserve these wonderful animals and their forest environment.

Farhani tells me that the best way we can help gorillas is to tell people about their plight. If enough people care, governments will listen and make sure that the gorillas and their mountain habitat will be protected.

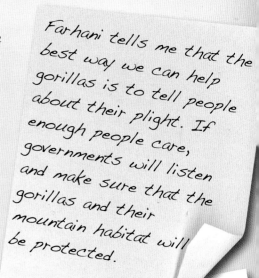

Rwanda is a poor country, and its people can benefit from the income provided by responsible gorilla tourism (see Guidelines on page 9). I hope that in the future the Rwandans will not need to destroy the rainforest for their livelihood.

Words to remember

Altitude The height of a place above sea level.

Bamboo A woody type of grass.

Blackback A male gorilla aged 6 to 10.

Deforestation The cutting or burning down of forests.

Forage To go looking for food.

Grooming Picking clean one another's body hair.

Habitat The place where a plant or animal naturally lives.

Immune system The body's natural defence against disease.

Parasite An animal or plant that lives in or on another animal or plant.

Poaching Illegal hunting or fishing.

Primates The group of animals that includes apes, monkeys and humans.

Rainforest An area with many different types of trees, where heavy rain falls during most of the year.

Reserve A place where wildlife is officially protected.

Silverback A fully grown male gorilla.

Weaned No longer needing its mother's milk.

Index